ESL or YOU WEREN'T HERE

ESL or YOU WEREN'T HERE

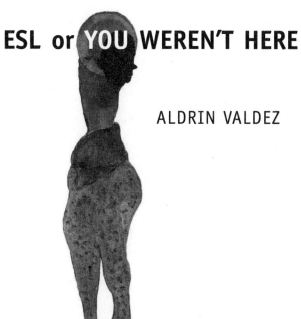

ALDRIN VALDEZ

NIGHTBOAT BOOKS
NEW YORK

ISBN 978-1-937658-86-1

Design and typesetting by Margaret Tedesco
Text set in Officina Sans and Sabon

Cover images by Aldrin Valdez
Front, *Inside Space (To Jax)*, 2012, (detail) mixed-media on paper
Back, *Inside Space (Child)*, 2014, (detail) mixed-media on paper

Cataloging-in-publication data is available from the Library of Congress

Nightboat Books
New York
www.nightboat.org

To Regina Feliciano Valdez

CONTENTS

ISA

Tagalog

Nanay once joked that when it came time to move to the U.S.
she'd beg the pilot to turn back. Or she'd jump out of the plane

swim back to Manila.

Come back

I pray

langoy

   langoy

langoy ka.

Swim with the river.

Sa ilog.

Taga ilog.

From the river.

Tagalog: People of the River.

   Nanay

  emerges from the water, cursing

the trash and tae floating all around her, clinging to her ill-fitting
dress, something she'd only ever wear to who knows—maybe an
embassy, to a stuffy plane full of 'kanos & balikbayans-to-be.

She twists her hair dry, a gesture her arms have memorized wringing wet fabric ten times as thick down the street from her house where neighbors gossiped over laundry.

She thinks to get on a jeepney, but she doesn't want to stink up the whole bus with the shitty water drying on her skin and clothes.

PUÑETA!

LECHE!

Tagalog curses feel good on her tongue.

She spits on the earth & begins to walk the many, many miles back to Tondo. She is used to walking.

The skin on her callused heels is a map of broken streets & syllables that fall like rain water on newly paved asphalt

i sa

da la wa

tat lo

a pat

li ma

a nim

pi to

wa lo

si yam

sam pu

Blue Bakla

isa

Contrary

to what I've been made to believe most of my life,

I am not   empty.

The air is full of water and someone's

hand pricks at it with a needle.

The water rushes out.

I panic.

Water is sadness

pulsing

in thick waves, now unstoppable.

I'm scrambling and shouting at other people to run.

All my borders are soaked!

And worse

blue is seeping into yellow.

dalawa

When yellow meets blue

                it is a floral duster dress

        my grandmother's body fills in.

           But if you were to burrow

                                into the belly of her dress,
                           you would find endless layers
                              of patterned fabric

            and no body.

tatlo

My grandmother is my mother.

She is Nanay.

I am a child and I have lost her

at the gate of St. Mary's Academy in Manila.

The security guard
is a scowl in uniform
berating me:

Your lola has to leave.
Kaylangan niya magtrabaho.
Get inside!

apat

Behind the gate, black & white shapes move swiftly through the halls. The bleached statue of a haughty Virgin Mary in the courtyard punishes a snake under her marble foot. October is Rosary Month. Every morning we kneel on the red tiles, a student leading us in prayer over the loudspeaker.

                    I seem to always   be quiet.

      I am dumb.

          The teachers' befuddled stares confirm it

      but I am fine with that.

I don't want to be so visible in school.
I can't speak English and reading frustrates me.
I am learning at a slow pace.
Like Maria Makiling
                 turning
      herself
      into a mountain.
I am learning to speak

      from, alongside
                       silence, writing

             as   drawing   :

    a curve
                 in the air,
       my head
& name
             aloud,
   land,
       the trees,

         my feelings.

lima

                                                                The English

                language

is Mrs. Modesta's pockmarked skin and potato nose.

                                                                The English

                language

is Mrs. Modesta's electrocuted elocution:

Pleazzzze   *sit down.*
                         Zzzeee
                         is for zzzebra.
                         Manila iz where?
                         It eeezzz on the island of Luzzzon.

                                                                The English

                language

is the gray foot of an elephant protruding
from my mouth in the first sentence
I ever read out loud in Mrs. Modesta's English class.

anim

Christopher & I sit in the front row
He is my best friend.
We fondle each other and no one sees.

Two   little   baklas

in white & navy blue.
The girls on the other side
are always laughing.
I tried to speak
to Jasmine once but her friends taunted me because they thought
I had a crush on her and because my name resembles the name
Aladdin.

pito

When asked to do the sign of the cross in Bible class
I let my hand spider from my forehead to my chest
then to my shoulders.

I am wrong.

Out of nervousness
I have used my left hand.

I am asked to repeat.

When we aren't praying, we are drawing
images of Jesus Christ.

      Mine is a man in a mandorla
radiating stars & ribbons of light.

Or we're making lists of who has talked in class while the teacher is out of the room.

Ma'am! Ma'am!

We would rush to her

tattling the names of classmates.

walo

Christopher and I love to sing
Mariah Carey's *Without You.*
Christopher says over the phone that he has never sounded so good
as he does now.
I agree with him.
His voice has the motion of a wilting
gumamela shaking
under the breath of a kambing.

I, on the other hand, when I get home from school, am an exceptional singer.

I sing   everywhere.
                Into the electric fan.
                In the bathroom with the tabo in my hand.
                In front of a gathering of neighbors outside during brownouts.
I sing for attention and the more I get the more I sing.

My Tita Alice and I sing with my Ates and Kuya.
She stations us on top of tables and couches.
Bedsheets drape our bodies. When she points to each of us,

we emerge like caryatids from the sheets

        as Mariah
        & Whitney
        & Celine,

the fabric cascading to our furniture-turned-stages.

siyam

Mga kapatid ko say
I am   KSP: Kulang Sa Pansin.
When they're really trying
to make the pikon in me
come out they say
I am   KSP: Kulangot Sa Pader.

And I get flustered—
I am not lacking attention!
I am not a booger on the wall!

I am a huffed-up balloon of Tagalog curses—
which I promised
to Lord
Jesus Christ
I would
never,
ever
say
again

if he would just please save my family and me from hell?

A never-ending
litany
of saviors, saints, & the prospective saved
lulls me to sleep each night like a pacifier.

sampu

But it is Nanay who rescues me
from the tukso of my Kuya and Ates.

Nanay is dilaw ng manga in an asul morning.
The rustling of the plastic bag she unfurls

is also the wrinkled, brown skin
of her hand as she offers me a mango.

I have missed dinner and she wakes me up now
and takes me outside where it is so blue

even the air seems colored-in
& the yellow of the mango hums in this blue.

The Albularyo

Remembering is a nebulous blue breathing. There is this side and many other sides. Tagalog words filter through with little English clouds attached to them. LUMALAKAD is a cumulous puff: *walking*, across a serrated sky. I trip on its ridges. HINDI is not a rain cloud as one might expect, but many wisps of cirrus. Surprisingly fair weather for a *NO*. But, on my knees, I see the sky as the blank white of *without*, WALA. I hear a voice proclaim: *breathing is the connection between what you can & cannot control.*

One day I wake up without my legs.

The floor is cold.
Pain shoots from base of spine, punishing when ambulates, stands, rigid, quaky, down.
I lean on the wooden arm of the sofa, late for school.
My Ates and Kuya hurry about in their uniforms.
My grandmother folds the blankets we'd been sleeping on.

Nanay, my voice crackles towards her. *I can't get up.*

In the morning, there

is this tongue

& many other

tongues. Still,

borders

circumscribe:

Nanay in Manila.

Mama in America.

Between them,

oceans.

You didn't have polio, Mama explains over the phone. *You had something else.*

But how could she

know

and shouldn't she

know?

All those years,

she was away.   And even if

I didn't have polio,

my family in the Philippines

still used the word

to name

my inability

to walk or to walk without

pain.

Just as we used

Colgate

to refer to any

tube of toothpaste.

                                        The   sky   opens   up.   Its
                                                                lumines
                                                                  cence
                                                                 stings.

The albularyo enters our house, where it is dark. She lights a candle.
I lie on the floor on a banig, a pillow under my head. My family
surrounds me. Their figures taper off to the dim corners of the house,
form a halo of warm silhouettes. The albularyo readies an aluminum
bowl of water. I am moved closer to her, causing pain to shoot down
my legs. What happened, what caused this? The albularyo pours
melted candle wax onto water. She's here to name the pain. The wax
hardens on the water's surface. Have you been around trees and plants
recently? Yes. Did you pick them? Yes. I had been out playing with
my cousin outside the school down the street, ripping grass blades
from the pavement, undoing the green seeds from their stems. You've
stepped on a duwende. What? A duwende witch. I look at the hardened
wax floating on water, imagine a duwende's outline emerging from
its soft rivulets. The albularyo massages oil onto my legs, and here I
cannot remember the pain. It is the word ANINO falling on my chest.
Shadows. Her touch is what I can sense. She heeds me apologize to
the duwende. With shame, I whisper sorries. Thumbs press below my
knees. The shadows evaporate, there is ease in my legs.

            Manang,

        How do I ask forgiveness from someone I can't see?

        (Tabi-tabi po.   Tabi-tabi po.)

        Will she hear me?

During a brownout:

I dream the mangkukulam's laugh is wedged between walls
of cinderblock. The passageway is narrow and cold.
I can't see her. I don't know why she laughs.
The dream dissipates before I can choose to enter.

Above Tondo, the flickers of shadow may be bats or a tik-tik
announcing its love like a parent's voice—so close
in your ear   on the phone   overseas.

Nanay cautions: Beware of dog-thieves looking for pulutan.
Poochie dies months later. Ate Amy & Ate Analyn bury her in a field
near the junkyard, where the grave they dig is too shallow,
the earth too dry. Drunk men find her,
cook her over a fire. The smell of burnt fur
covers the air for hours.

San Miguel is a bottle of pale lager sweating in the city heat.

The manangs warn: Do not point a finger at the moon, lest the spirits
notice you. Point with your lips instead.

Dead powerlines notwithstanding, the streets glow brilliant
with candles and gossip.

Somewhere, an aswang is a powerful woman refusing
to be beaten down, but the friars' education persists in us
centuries later, unbeknownst to us. We are born into
the fear of witches.

My Ate Amy says: If you see a friend without
a head, you must slap them so they don't die.

A folded diaryo counts as a pamaypay
no matter how urgent the news it carries.

Mama Mary appears to me in the mirror as a silhouette.
She is, it turns out, another mother without a face.

We learn, and re-learn, how to wait.

Crying makes the heat meaner, and Tatay, with his belt
undone, is tired.

Everybody has a good ghost story to tell
but not everybody feels safe enough to tell it.

I cling to Nanay as though she were bound to disappear any minute now.

Kuya Paeng gently claps isa, dalawa, tatlo...and the lights
go on, by kismet or clockwork, in each stacked house
blowing out holes in the dark. For a moment,
magic is a promise of softness.

Photograph Curling

My Ates, red hibiscus
in their mouths,
& my Kuya, a distant
mirror, who am I
among you,

outside? Beneath
a Manila sky
forever bleached, or am I
imagining it so:

white,
threatening—
Humidity,

a certain sadness
bearing down
on our little, brown
bodies.

•

na a a la la
u ma a poy
bu mu bu lak lak
ang
pa nga lan
ni
Na nay
gu ma me la
sa
u ma ga
sa
ga bi
ma di lim
na
ang
la ngit
ng
pu so

Her voice, an image,

              whisper- round, close

                              my earlobe,

                                      cochlear, deeper, below

                   my eyes. Then

                              nowhere near

                     me, removed

                 from me.

              It is removed.

                 Who moved it?

                    Where did it go?

          •

It's June 6 again,

My mother, newly returned after eight years,
is taking us back with her to New York. I'm at
the doorstep shouting goodbye to a neighbor.

My grandmother is behind me, on the sofa.
Just arrived from the hospital, she can barely
stand. She's here to see us off.

Her voice is the softest ligature, unthreading.

Why are you saying goodbye to everyone except for me who raised you?

DALAWA

Crossing

        She was
supposed
        to be here
would she
        angry
as she was
        have loved
me less
        in my
survival

        red
        white
        blue

would she
        have faded
as she did
        if she had
come here
        it would
have been
        no better
to die
        in America
her body
        angry
mine lost

        imagine

a coffin
        being
shipped
        back to
Manila

November

Nanay is dead.
Nanay is the gray
telephone. My head
is the holes
in the gray
telephone. My fingers
fit into the holes & hold
my eyes in place.
My back is where
the wall meets the carpet.
My Ates pour
out
the bedroom
down
the narrow corridor.
Blue jeans
smudge
blue walls.
My face
is Johnson's
baby powder
white.
Meant to scare them
hiding
in the corner
but November
entered
the room instead
& my Ates were crying.
My Kuya sleeps in the sofa.
We shake him wake up.
We shake him wake up.
She's gone.
Wake up.

Wake up to warm touching cold
breathing out the torn
open night.

Blue yellow blue yellow
fade.
HERE I AM
says the something you don't normally see.
In the blue
corridor
full of Mama's blue
saints
with their blue
always open
eyes.

Wake up to Papa
in the backyard
punching the cold trashcan.
Jean jacket shoulder.
Yellow dark.
Yellow dark.
Against the metal
clunk clunk.
To hide
his mother
gone.

Wake up the next day
to Atlantic City.
Mama & Papa's answer
to a long
distance
call.
Is still
never
and colder.
My Ates my Kuya & me
in a white numb car.

IN A WHITE NUMB CAR—
IN A WHITE NUMB CAR—
IN A WHITE NUMB CAR—

go my thumbs
on the gray machine
down the green tubes
to the submarine world
little red jumper man eating stars.

GRAYWHITEBLACK—
GRAYWHITEBLACK—
GRAYWHITEBLACK—

jumps the rain
thudding the car roof
flooding the street.
Yellow turns red
through graywhiteblack.
Diagonal clouds
fill curbside
brick building
traffic light.

Do not like Papa pointing
to an older woman
crossing in the rain.
Everyone agrees
she looks like her.
Holding breath
until red
stops
to go
again.
In the graywhiteblack
little wet companions
cross the road
clutching at her
raincoat tail.

Do not like toy machine
picking plush life still & soft
many tiny things
will be dirtied soon
or dirty already.

Do not like
casino
cigarette
smoke
the rain
pelts
the car
into mist.

YOU ARE NOT THE COLD GRAY

says the rain
but the window wiper right
to left
to leaving
her
behind.

fall / pall

It's a Friday when she's gone.

In Manila, her leaving is faster: 12 hours into Saturday—
in New York, does that mean she is still alive?

Beg the impossible for a slip in time & language:
Leaving. A leaving. Let her spirit travel.
A clock, a leaf. Autumn, her body a duster dress
of foliage. Autumn, a mother. Leaving, the sky.

Is it too much to ask that a telephone call be taken back?
Explain you don't want it at all. Leaves don't whir,
don't fit inside a phone. They turn color & fall, as they should,

so a figure may form on the ground, because there *is* a ground.

A child must not be bereft. See: the leaves shape a mother,
layered brown, orange, yellow, red. Her face, the most colorful.

Heed the sun stay longer. Stay, crepuscular, warm her bones.

ESL or You Weren't Here

bago ang lahat ay pahalik at payakap

Back to school & new pronouns.
The side by side of SISTER & BROTHER
as if all born together instead of the looking
up & watching over of ATE & KUYA.

I am a HE now.
HE gets the words confused ALOT.
ALOT—*NO—RE-*
MEMBER—A LOT is A LOT of words.

Brittany I say. It's Monday, her curls beautiful & American.
We're in the playground wearing puffy jackets.
Pebbles scatter on asphalt.

My grandmother just died.

She doesn't believe me.
Says why are you in school then if she died.

o kumusta ka na ngayon diyan

White lace beneath the Virgin Mary
& the rosy cheeks of the Santo Niño
resemble
my grandmother
atop a dresser
welcoming me home
in the corridor
under dusty light.

She tells me not to hurry.
My shoes in my hands.
There are leaves outside.
Why is no one picking them up?

Nobody is at the corridor,   silly.

Nanay will never come to America.

sana ay gumaling ako para makita ko kayo uli

Nobody is outside singing.

No New Year's Eve fireworks to send me running

up the stairs
        into her arms petaling
open
            like jasmines
                    in her duster dresses.

Fireworks I hate
but I love the shape
I become
in her arms.

                'Nay

            I say as she sinks into the sofa through the floor—

magpakabait ka anak ko malayo ako

Nanay I say

    She's a cartoon now

        visiting me through the windows
        as real as purple

                She's a pinstripe suit

                  Who are you?

                She's wearing a fedora

    'Nay I say   something's wrong huh?

    I don't hear her disagree

    the window is a burst   of yellow

    'Nay I say & don't
    wake up

    She's a curtain
    in my eyelids

dear aldrin rey

bago ang lahat ay pahalik at payakap

o kumusta ka na ngayon diyan

sana aldrin ay gumaling ako para makita ko
kayo uli

magpakabait ka anak ko malayo ako

the moon is big & blue

the night is beautiful

*the boy in the haystack and the sheep in the meadow are
fast asleep*

who will say goodbye now? not I, not I says the moon

Mrs. B Tells My Mother I Must Speak Only English at Home

NEARBY is not pronounced as NEAR-BE.
GRANDMOTHER is GRANDMOTHER
only.

Admit NANAY contains two negatives.
Yes, also NIGH,
as in ALMOST HERE,
but the word is ARCHAIC,
meaning
FAR
AWAY IN TIME
or NO
LONGER.

Abandon
PRIMITIVE
attachments.

My teachers, mother
remind me,

You're in America now.

Long Distance Images

Wake Photograph 1

Kuya shows me the long distance photographs
of the funeral past my curfew.
I can't sleep. My eyelids stream the gray photographs.
I am everywhere in the wake. I am Tita Bombit's hair
as she leans over the coffin. My cousins wear black
rectangles over their hearts.

Wake Photograph 2

The photograph is Nanay's gray face. The light is glass
over her eyes. The coffin is one long sampaguita strand.
Her hands are under where I can't see them.
I am thousands of miles away.

Wake Photograph 3

When I close my eyes I am my cousins Paul & Jenny
Ace Lalaine Sarah Eunice MaeMae being lifted over
the coffin from one pair of hands to another to ward
off haunting. I am the neighbors carrying the coffin. I
am Morong Street. I have never walked this far from
home. It is so crowded.

Wake Photograph 4

I am the sampaguita lining the door of her coffin. I am not
the light that streaks across the glass, creates
a glare.
Please don't let me be the glare.
I want to be the sampaguita.

January

I am baffled by before & after. January is a new word
without her. November is still here though.

Tatay 1

And Tatay arriving from Manila. He's in the corridor
now a tan jacket black & red plaid lining the inside.
Promises he'd made to Nanay fall out like coins.

To follow. To America. To take care of us.

He sleeps in the living room. Bootleg Lion King plays
on VHS. A haze obscures the edges. All the characters
are far away as if seen from across a very big room in
a very big, empty house. I don't realize I am waiting for
people to arrive onscreen & rescue the little animals.

Hospital Photograph

There are times when she is still living interspersed
with gray & glare. There she is. In the hospital bed.
A droopy wrist.
Her youngest son, my Tito Rick, a messy laugh. Did he cry
later after this photograph?
The sight of tubes in her nose. Her beautiful brown skin
against impending white walls.

Image Anatomy

Nanay bathing puppies in a plastic tub
out in pavement. The sun an entire feeling.
This isn't a photograph but my shoulders.

Tatay 2

Tonight Tatay is sleeping in the black vinyl rocker in the living room cursing the Japanese. There are bullets falling on his toes. It's a long time ago tonight.

Winter Fever

A feeling like a hand in my throat growing sleepless into new year. Heavy blue velvet curtains the orange carpet. Mama & Papa move me out to the living room so my Ates and Kuya won't get sick.

I make my parents laugh with fever antics.
Delicious I say. The cough syrup burning but sweet late at night.

Living Room Photograph 1

She's alive again resting on the sofa her feet blurry. Tatay reads to her while cousins smile at the camera, populate like bright little trees the new linoleum floor.

Detail 1

In all the photos the décor has changed from when I used to live there. Now there's a new couch new floors new curtains.

Living Room Photograph 2

She wears a rosary, rests on diagonal layers of pillows. A light shapes Tatay's round knee as he reads to her.

Detail 2

Is she clasping letters are those bills meds instructions
prayers?

Her hand

her leaving

a breath escapes

or our leaving her—

You are not the same

person

when she leaves,

or you leave.

How can you

be,

when her sound moved in your

body, years and no   longer, but   each organ remembers.

Perhaps. Each organ has

a soul.

Hers   inhabits, embraces

yours.

You could say

She's been here all along.

How hurt follows   then, its little fingers

searching.

How stupid,

how angry,

    it makes you.

        Where is she?

Where is she?

The easy answer is *here*.

      Sternum beneath

      hand & the heart

      blood below.

Here.

The hardest to hold.

TATLO

Purple Gender

In the red room stands a purple gender
a nervous color.
Me. Surrounded.

I remember when I was circumcised.
I counted down to one.
I was not alone but I was without—the *right* context?

Is that it? What is a right context for cutting out—

I miss my foreskin.
Not its added length
but its petal-ness.

I was 10 and summer on the boardwalk was a bright contusion of sunlight. Afternoon and my mother held my hand. This was my context. Everything was set to go for surgery in the following week. It was like a gift. She took me to Burger King after a visit to the doctor's and we walked home. So visible & together. Just me & her. A rare occasion because another afternoon she would have been sleeping, having worked all night. She wouldn't be holding my hand.

I felt special. Soon I would be...a man? Or readying to be a man? Somewhere down the line past 10. Manhood. Its color, a pale that tans. Elvis-white & hard.

Not me though.

Not mine.

I remember my brother & cousins. Together,

          my Kuyas. They must have also been around 10.

Manila. It was *their* context. It should have been mine also.

If I had had no choice but   to be cut, I would rather
it
was under a   different
sun, in another set of   hands.
But *whose*

hands?   / A memory trembles,
could be wrong, but vividly
          like skin

it plays. After my Kuyas were circum /

cised they wore   skirts.

Or was this just a threat in / cised   into my mind?

Do not be soft.

Do not be open.

At the edge of openness: humiliation.

But what an image. I cherish it.

Boys in skirts.

If this happened, was it to humiliate them in front of the older boys &

      men? Or to take

care of them? A skirt opening

more space
    in which to heal.

In the elevator, the tall white doctor says the word

      titi

 referring to mine.

      titi

It's tiny coming from him & silly.

I laugh behind my hands.

My mother stands next to me. I ask her

why the doctor is using that word.

It's because he thinks you can't speak English.

But I can.

Well you aren't speaking.

(In memory a translation

takes place whether we spoke

English or Tagalog. My mother's

voice flickers.

It is hers & no longer

hers. I grow

small, behind

my hands.)

On the operating table, I am asked by surgeons what I want to be when I grow up. They remark on my name. Its origin. A white man on the moon. They are counting down. I am drifting off.

Do you want to be an astronaut?

The first Filipina to win the Miss Universe pageant
was Gloria Diaz in 1969. She was 18.

Now, you speak English well, I know that.

Miss Philippines,
in the next day or so a man will land on the moon. If a man
from the moon landed in your hometown, what would you do
to entertain him?

> *Oh. Uh. It's the same things I do. After he's been*
> *on the moon for so long, I think when he comes*
> *over he wants to change, I guess.*

Very good. Very good, Miss Philippines.

The ancestral sense of HOLD is preserved in BEHOLD: "to keep, to tend, to watch over" / see: HAPTIC / see: "a place of refuge" / see: where?

I
remember
in the mornings
my hand
between
my legs
a mosquito
bite swelled
the foreskin
to a pout
round-succulent
gumamela-mollusk
bulb-bulaklak
pistil-brown
swole
a soft heaviness buoyant in fingers
before waking before other names
could seep & fix
I held myself

The white
urologist
does not contain
his laughter
as he holds
my genitals
during a checkup.
I am not a man. I am
quiet as he advises me
to press the fat above my groin
so that the _____
can appear
longer, more permanent
in its protrusion.
I am eleven.
He advises.
I see
years
ahead of me,
the work of pressing down,
of growing bigger, of full blunt force,
getting harder. Of diminishing softness. Little *i*
as in *i would rather my hands than his*
but in this moment I do not hold
myself. Measured,
I am lacking.
The carpet in his
office is a gray thick tweed
probably synthetic
though as prickly
as real
wool.

Divination with Utensils

If a spoon falls   a woman

will

enter the room. If

a fork   falls

a man will

enter the room.

And if a knife. Should visit. Your body. The room. The day. Cuts. Clean. The child-yawn. Morning. Slanting through. And language. Like a star. You wish. Had fallen. Into your whole. Heart. And so. To speak. All. Four. Rooms. Of it. Beating. A red color. A red color. Out into. The blue. Day. Of someone else's. Yes. Someone. Else's yes. But. No. No. No. Implores. My whole. Heart. Do not. Enter. Do not enter.

P / Ph / F

I can't find the newspaper account online of a Pilipino who cut off his own penis. I know I didn't make it up. It was the late 90s. My family subscribed to a Filipino newspaper whose name eludes me now. I remember the newspaper's name was in bold, red letters. Online, I find the New York-based *Filipino Reporter*, also bold & red. I type PENIS, MUTILATION in the search bar. Ten results come up but none about the Pilipino who cut off his own penis.

The *Filipino Reporter*'s tagline is FAIR, FEARLESS, FACTUAL.

Lately I've been identifying myself as PILIPINO and PINOY, and become conflicted as to when to use the terms and, in conversation, with whom.

The Filipino.

The Pilipino.

When I was a child, how long did it take me to learn to pronounce words that began with *F* and *PH*?

I am PROM the PEELEEPEENS.

I am PAIR, PEARLESS, PACTUAL.

The parenthetical of my shame
cups words like a mother
clutching to her chest something fragile
or forbidden,
in a hurry to a white doctor
who will deem the brown flesh she holds
as irreparably damaged.

It was a (touch) & go situation.

The (man) had (cut) off his (own) (penis).

He and his (family) may have lived in Queens.

I unquestioningly imagined the ER doctor who saw them as (white).

He spoke (English).

Was the article in (English) or (Tagalog)?

Or in (Tagalog) with smatterings of (English), as when the doctor spoke?

The (son) had cut off his (own) (penis).

His (mother) found him.

She may have been accompanied by an (aunt).

He was not coherent.

The doctor expressed dismay at the (mother) and (aunt's) decision to place the (penis)
in a container of (rubbing) (alcohol) and ice.

In her panic, she had (grabbed) her (son's) dismembered (penis).

She asked her sister to fetch a cup or maybe it was a small cooler.

To fill it with ice and (rubbing) (alcohol).

Was the (penis) surrounded by the ice or did it lie atop the ice, bathed in (rubbing) (alcohol)?

[I realize I have been (fleshing) out the image without blood.

Thus—]

The (rubbing) (alcohol) turned red, and the ice.

The doctor expressed dismay (in English) at the (mother) and (aunt's) decision to place
the (penis) in a container of (rubbing) (alcohol) and ice.

He may have said the ice was a wise decision, but the (rubbing) (alcohol) was not.

The (rubbing) (alcohol) made it impossible to save the (penis).

The (penis) could not be re-(attached).

Photograph

Once, my grandfather showed me a photograph. His mother's burial. In the ground, a hole, the casket splayed open. She, as though sleeping vertically. Her family flanking the rectangle of the grave, the grave framing the rectangle of the coffin. I can't remember whether my grandfather said his mother was Portuguese or Spanish. Telling you this I hold my breath, release it around the Tagalog word *puti*, imagining more photographs I may never see. My grandfather, a brown Filipino, fought alongside Americans against the Japanese but was not granted the citizenship he was promised until his 70s, after my grandmother had died from cancer in Manila, unable to join him when eventually he immigrated to the States. There are days when this fact twists my breathing and a single, stark detail pulses within the still image—not of the photograph, but of the memory of the photograph: the silver white hair of my grandfather's mother shimmering against the dead, dull dirt. Had it been a lighter color when she was younger? Was it black, brown, light brown. Blond? How far back is a pale color? I marvel at my family's invisible lineages. How, in our blood, our ancestors must still clash and kill one another, divide and come together & love,   baffled.

Opened

Purple Gender in the bathtub; the door unlocked.
How the older boys find him: Purple Gender wondering
if the door is locked. They enter & the tiles catch
laughter & the water hitting Purple Gender
catches laughter. On his body is laughter,
sharp staccato between his legs, water
laughing louder now.

Why are they hurting me like so: his cries caught
in the water's tiled laughter.
They leave him be but this is how it starts.
Another day the older boys come back
& Purple Gender is taken unawares.
But Purple Gender fights the passive voice:
They took him unawares.
Yes, they took him unawares.
Purple Gender in this telling is telling you
they took him unawares into his sister's bedroom.

They took him unawares at the door.

Purple Gender kicking, kicking.

Laughter

kicking back a great, rude gallop.
Purple Gender laughs, too, at first,   so muddled
in his chest head body whole   body

muddled.   He kicks

stomps

screams

STOP

but Purple Gender's knees are finger joints
flicking in comparison.

Why are the older boys doing this? Aren't they his family, his friends?

Purple Gender as still-life, thus: spread open, shorts down,

life distilled to an image repeating:

They spread his legs open
& the camera opens
its wide eye;
the older boys pin
Purple Gender open,
spread-eagled,
& the camera opens
its wide eye,
shuttering:
its wide eye opened,
swallowing light:
the smallness between
Purple Gender's legs:
a still-life photograph

This is not a self-portrait.

This is not a self-portrait,
Purple Gender
yells at you.

They took him unawares & made him so aware. Made him so aware of
how his legs opened. Made him so aware of negatives & the glossy skin
of photographs, returning from the camera shop. Made him so aware
of other people looking without him knowing. Made him so aware of
his mother at the table looking through the photos, just arrived, tucked
between candid faces. Made him memorize her voice when she said,

You shouldn't let them do that to you.

Memory

Darkness between my legs. Several browns enfold.

I want him to ask gently so I may say yes and stay

the whole time through. In sex, my spirit is not

an aura that tapers off, leaves, hovers above bed.

No. I refuse the weight of danger. Instead my history

is a matter of choice—mine. I say, stop your gnarled

rippling and the memories listen. They are not

photographs, rather a matter of nerves. Or they are

photographs and a matter of nerves. I want to learn

so the circuit doesn't loop against me: memory as matter.

The mind tries to hold but memory keeps transforming.

Pleated skirt like palm leaves I slip off. We are very

slow together, introducing parts to parts. Blood rushes.

Flesh goes hard so it may be more fully held. I want this

to be a healing. I would rather cry than come

but can we do both?

Bumigay

     delineates the collapse of a structure once believed to have been stable, stoic,
say, a house, disarranged, revealed fraudulent, rotting.
A weakness in the rigor of a wall.
Or the hip, in contrapposto,
curving the body's gaze towards another,
in pathetic, petal desire.

                           Your wrist going

               limp.

On you,

     SHAME.   SHAME.   SHAME

                         on you,

    You couldn't keep it together? Couldn't hold it all inside?

        Gave up.

Gave in.

        BADING.

        BAKLA.

      BIBIG   becoming   BUNGANGA,

an organ   without   humility.

I admit my loneliness, a certain solitude's unsteady constitution.

On the night D, one of our Pinoy friends since that first year in America,
posted a photo of his gun on Facebook, threatening one of my sisters,

I was lonely.

D had gone to high school with my siblings, had spent countless days at our house,
had been like another older brother, a Kuya.

(I fixate on this fact of family, as though it should save us, as though the home
were immune to violence and not an originator of violence.)

My sister had told D's wife he'd been cheating on her,
gave her the name of the other woman.

Now D points a gun in the comment section.

In his rage, he involves my brother, his best friend in adolescence, and me.

BUMIGAY daw kami. He claims. My brother & me: BUMIGAY.

The two of us—as though united—rather than separated by—collapsed into—
our queernesses.

As if there were something noble in staying still, in denying the articulation
of breath,
in silence—or rather, in being *silenced*.

In depriving ourselves the life force to say, finally, I love, I am loved.

We are capable, in these ways:

My brother with his husband.

And I with—?   I with—I   with—   I—

                              I—

         I—

I shut the lights off

in case
D drives by.
I'm crying. (Was I
crying.) I'm shaking.
I'm so afraid. Of
what. Shaken. By the
night. Of the image
of the gun. The gun
spinning. The gun
breaking the window.
D cursing at us, his
spit, the gun, spitting,
the bullets entering
the house, me. The
screen, the computer,
the phone, my face,
  shattering. His
 car,
thunderous. The door
I've locked & relocked. And I.
Myself. Panicking into the phone. Must have called my sisters.
All three. Each one reasoning, D wouldn't truly hurt us. He's
just—*ANGRY, CONFUSED*—And me? I dial again, this time
the police. I'm alone in my family's house, the blinds are drawn,
broken, the curtains sheer. I—*I* stammer—I—splinter in my
voice—*I*—deviant interior—my queerness made known—a
busted mouth—a hole of further holes.

Wearing a skirt on a Sunday afternoon

what's under there

        hollering whispers

                conjoined stares

around the corner

            no
            no
            no
            no
            no

how do you expect to be treated seriously as a man if you're dressed like that—

(quietly:

I DON'T

I REALLY

REALLY

DON'T)

Faggot Phonetics

Fricative:
                Breath.

                        Rubbed.

                                        Through body.
                                                    opening.

                                                                e.g.
                                            Lips, teeth, tongue
                                                    narrowing
                            the passage of air as it exits the mouth.

                                    If
                        in the doorway,
                                    I.
                        In the doorway,
                                    I
                            an If.

The wind rushes around my arms, between my legs.
Consonant gust in the shape of the negative of my body enters.

Enters.
Enters.
Enters.

This house where I am mother sprung from my tongue.
I   cross-tailed, hands akimbo.
At the place of articulation,

                        pleasure.

O faggotry in the fuchsia of my brain.

Vroom-eared, valiant bakla am I, abuzz in my soft, soft.

I speak a scream muscle, throat & trill.

When you say my name:

Roll the R.

Sagad

In my hand your genitals: your words

tangled, thick hair, your lovely, uncut—

I ask permission to name—

cock, you permit—

& it enters & leaves, enters

& leaves, enters & leaves—I

am breathing. Mourning comes

in little waves as desire comes

in little waves: O—to let my mouth

be a site for feeling!

In Tagalog, I tell you, *there's a word*

for this fullness—Sagad: to the hilt,

as in a sword or a screw.

And just like that, violence

punctures the field of conversation.

But let it be transmutable, as when you,

sagad in me, say *ram & ride*,

I think of clouds above Manila

with its sky-flung blue, & sweat,

a tropic bloom city street folded metal

          painted Virgin Mary palm-prayer pink—

The breath moves, pain

          moves along with it. My throat,

then the branches of my lungs. Soon

          the disembodiment the act of naming

can be, gives way to the warm

          fogginess of staying, a slow,

low atmosphere. Here. In this body,

          as it meets your body, there is a rhythm

like knowing & unknowing,

          asking, then waiting to be answered.

Once, my kiss wasn't with lips

          but with an O'Hara poem I fumbled

in the dark, half-memorized, to you.

          To be the child in the poem, weeping

in the bathtub, just as lost, but feeling okay

          with not returning to myself, as myself was,

just a few moments ago, before I,

          longing, kissed you.

SHUFFLED SLIDES OF A CHANGING PAINTING

89.

You're still too close for me to write this.

Listen,

I whisper in the subway

where a ghost of you   passes in my periphery.

"There are landslides—

I'm so corny!" I laugh, hiding my tears under a hoodie. Stevie Nicks woke me up one morning and I was very young.

How does it go?
Something about mirrors.

Mountains.

Listen.

Now you tumble out of view,   gone.

4.

The clacking sound we hear is no typewriter but a carousel of slides.
Its images   puddle on the wall,

absorb themselves.
One into the other.

                                        Into the other.

                                                                Into

the other.

My hand

                                in yours,

                                a color & a set of bones.

33.

My chest dissolves into

      stairs   forest   cage

an explanation settles

      briefly as breath rustling

a room at six p.m.

      I've been in bed all day

I swallow my own voice

60.

A sore point between shoulder blades   is a keyhole to a flooded room

85.

Around us, the bar is way too loud. You play with my
tattered cuff as I speak. I'm reading from my phone.

This poem. Which is different now.

2.

"You drifted by" could be one beginning.

Another: "This isn't working."

And another: "It didn't work out."

47.

I feel heavy   holding my breath.

I light a candle and remember   what kind of saint

                                                  Michael the Archangel

was. I would really like

                to open my back & drape my lungs over my shoulders.

Can he make me that strong that I become soft?

                                        Alveoli,
                                                alveoli,
                                                        alveoli wings.

6.

And so the projections continued. I tried not to scold
my childself. Unruly as they are   (*they*,

> because there was no *he* or *she* yet,
> at least not in the Tagalog words I spoke)

They-child,

shaking the shadows for a familiar body, changing you
from someone I could get to know

to *a person who is about to leave*
or has already left.

Hoy bata!   I tell that self, you try so hard not to feel

> abandoned.
> & I remember

them, queer, bakla, phaeton-like, staring at the Manila sun one morning
as though they could see more than its yellow haze.

> Perhaps,
>
> as in darkness, searching
>
> in light for a body their body
>
> remembered.

10.

You know, my mother
apologized. I asked her to listen
and I could feel her press
closer into the phone.

Buksan mo yung chest mo, she said.

I misheard, anticipating her anger.

Your chest,

she permitted. & so
for 30 minutes I wailed.

Two decades:

she was there : she wasn't there.

73.

And what would you have me do?

said Eurydice.

12.

Mama immigrated to New York by herself.

Whiling away the days
until my father could join her,

she dreamed

each

passing

plane

was the one

carrying him

to JFK.

34.

The wallpapers in the museum
are loud with images that defy
and demand   language.

Sometimes:

                                                                    I feel like

a white man   & then: *This is some other*

                                                    queer's loss.

By which I think I mean I am tired.

                                        I've grown

                    skilled   in cruising for my story

where my story does not exist.

30.

A lonely binary

is a switchblade

        snapping   the body   open / shut :

am   I   learning to love

           or aspiring

    to whiteness?

86.

The dissolution of come in soapy water as I remember you.

29.

Sometimes we talked and my whole self
was a downward gaze.

14.

White gay boy,

       tell me you feel as lost & too full
                    of meaning as I do moving
                    from room to room of collided
                    histories, those that collide
                    because we have been taught
                    to see them piecemeal.

65.

AIDS is not separate from 9/11 and yet why does my mind take leaps?
A sink carries water but, elongated, a body too;

                          half-sunk in dirt, a sign for no longer.

& just a few floors above us, Matisse's *The Red Studio*,
painted in 1911, compels one's eyes to enter what is otherwise a flat surface and,
haptically, to behold

                          a chair drawn this way, a clock.

59.

am I being unreasonable
by demanding that I should always be
embodied

/

So needy, so angry
went the block & tackle
pulling tighter

tighter.

68.

1899

in your blue
eyes. You don't know.
It's not fair maybe, to look,
but I see it there. How much of the past
I let overtake me, how much of the present
I deny.

61.

To say   so much loss precedes us   is to ask, where

in this prone body   does each—leaving, expanding

                          bullet, pacific-

ation, fire, water-cure, bomb, march, English

word—reside?

16.

I'm still waiting for her to return

is *a borderline* in my brain.

No medical terms, please.

Send another word

to light up the room where she isn't.

She isn't coming back

        stumbling
    down
my spine

like the wooden stairs of our house on Morong Street.

77.

On Allen Street, the cold isn't so bad

                  for a moment. A green surprise—palm

leaves spread like hands

                  on frosted pavement. Des'ree sings

I'm Kissing You & I mistake the clock

                  in the clock tower for a full moon.

A stranger on the train unknowingly

                  grazes the small of my back. I want to tell

them, please, stay, touch

                  the bones of your wrist to my spine.

84.

I press my ear then lips to your

pelvis to listen to a scar to feel

what you remember

                              then if

it's okay   to heal together.

67.

In English class, Ms. Rios cancels the air with her hands
as she describes the Twin Towers

                                                  falling. The sky is blue.

I'm running by the water

in Long Beach, turning to face west,

                                  my mouth parched with words:

                                  American, horizon, citizen,

                                  who—

                         /

And where were you when it happened?

You tell me: out in the woods by your house, farther east in Smithtown.
You'd asked your mother if you could play there with your friends.

The buildings are nowhere
in sight. You know
but do not know.

53.

I roll the R now when I say my name

                    it's like I'm biting on pearls apologetically.

50.

Once, a man came to school to speak
about HIV & AIDS. He was poz. After
his talk, he entered the bathroom & I
followed. I didn't know this was called
cruising. I just had so many questions.
Not in words. I watched my desires
from afar as if I were a window pointed
inward.
On the other side of the stall,

                    his   sound
becoming

        a shape

        I wanted

to hold.

24.

I become the etymology of intimate.

Intimare.   To put or bring into.
                      To make familiar.

Intimus.   Inmost. Innermost.

17.

"My grandmother was my mother"

sounded so queer growing up
I had to translate the story out of shame
& ESL so that my American friends could
understand my Tagalog trauma.

/

I can't
tell a memory from a wish,
or if it even matters.

Her duster dresses

are my arms folding tightly around her waist during an
earthquake in Manila. And later. When it is calmer. Or
there is just more silence. She repeats. A word. Over &
over. Pleading beneath the dining table. Each utterance
deepening a prayer.

28.

Nearer the surface, it was harder to discern between shadow and mishap. There was a longing for words like *truth* / *in the end* / *palpable* / *clearly* / *overcome* /

self. A flickering, like light or heat, made the both of

them—*him*

turn and Orpheus glimpsed the depth of all that loss. How alone he'd been, then again, not so alone, after all. How that could be, he wasn't sure. Slowly, a hurt making space: not alone, but lonely, a body that didn't know how to hold a mind injured by contradictions. In the distance / inside / long ago / once / again, he saw him

self in pieces, mangled, many.

3.

And still,

        and still,

        and still.

Another beginning could go like this:

            You held my hand.
            The painting changes.

Notes

The section titles in the poem *ESL or You Weren't Here* and the same words that appear in the poem *dear aldrin rey* are excerpts from the only surviving, and most likely the last, letter I received from my grandmother in Manila after my siblings and I had moved to the U.S.

The lines "the boy in the haystack and the sheep in the meadow are / fast asleep" are re-phrasings of lines from the poem "Little Boy Blue" by Mother Goose.

The exchange from the Miss Universe pageant host and Gloria Diaz is my transcription from a YouTube video excerpt.

The title of the poem *The ancestral sense of HOLD is preserved in BEHOLD: "to keep, to tend, to watch over" / see: HAPTIC / see: "a place of refuge" / see: where?* is partially taken from, and a mash-up of, entries for the word "HOLD" in the Online Etymology Dictionary.

Shuffled Slides of a Changing Painting is inspired by Robert Gober's "Slides of a Changing Painting," a mixed-media work I saw during his 2014 retrospective at the Museum of Modern Art in New York. The work consists of 89 35-mm slides projected onto a white wall. Each slide depicts a stage of a painting on panel that Gober continuously worked on and painted over from 1982 to 1983. When presented as slides, the series of images created a kind of staggered animation of a torso in metamorphosis. I don't recall any specific order as the slides played repeatedly during museum hours. As such, a viewer may enter and exit the presentation at any given time and not feel compelled to assign a definitive narrative sequence to the images. By "shuffling" the poems that emerged in response to Gober's images, I sought to similarly eschew a linear and totalizing narrative for the gracious form of fragments.

Acknowledgments

Poems in *ESL or You Weren't Here* first appeared in earlier forms in the following publications: Belladonna*'s chaplet series, *Femmescapes*, *The Felt*, *Nat Brut*, *Poor Claudia*, and *The Recluse*. Thank you to the editors and curators who gave these words their first home and, by doing so, encouraged more writing. To the Nightboat team, thank you! To Andrea Abi-Karam, Lindsey Boldt, Stephen Motika, & Margaret Tedesco—for your labor, insight, and patience.

I am filled with gratitude toward my friends and community of visual artists, writers, and makers of all kinds. Thank you for your compassion, for bringing people together, for opening doors, for reading, for seeing, for listening, for asking, for texting, for calling, for calling out, for inviting, for dinner, for waiting, for writing back, for teaching, for dancing with me:

Miriam Atkin, Felipe Baeza, Amy Sayre Baptista, Kay Ulanday Barrett, Jmae Barrizo, Mariam Bazeed, Rijard Bergeron, Sébastien Bernard, BGSQD, Ella Boureau, Diana Cage, Emmy Catedral, Wo Chan, Cathy Linh Che, Alexis Clements, Devon Collins, Rio Cortez, Maxe Crandall, Jackson Davidow, Natalie Diaz, Arisleyda Dilone, Raychelle Duazo, Carolyn Ferrucci, Zachary Frater, Max Freeman, Cassidy Gardner, Phoebe Glick, Camilo Godoy, Rachel Eliza Griffiths, Nez Hafezi, John Hanning, Aimee Herman, Ian Hinonangan, Hayat Hyatt, Kiam Marcelo Junio, Rami Karim, Deborah Kass, Ted Kerr, Nikki Kurt, Joseph O. Legaspi, Rachel Levitsky, Ian Lewandowsky, Esther Lin, Charles Long, Lara Lorenzo, Jimena Lucero, Jackie Mariano, Andriniki Mattis, Vikas Menon, Saretta Morgan, Simon Moritz, Carrie Moyer, Mitchyll Mora, Cristobal Guerra Naranjo, Maggie Nelson, Lee Ann Norman, Kris Nuzzi, Geoff Olsen, Noam Parness, Sheila Pepe, PJ Policarpio, Chana Porter, Risa Puleo, Q/A/M folks, Edwin Ramoran, Elroy Red, Jasmine Reid, L.J. Roberts, Amy Sadao, Sarah Sala, Metta Sáma, Nelson Santos, Cecily Schuler, Sarah Schulman, Reema Sharma, James Sherry, Buzz Slutzky, Jayson P. Smith, Pamela Sneed, Stacy Szymaszek, Michael Tikili, R.A. Villanueva, the Visual AIDS fam, Adrien Weibgen, Josh Wizman, K. Wynn, and Yanyi.

Thank you especially to my sisters in poetry, in brownness, in queerness, in loss & healing: Ricardo Hernandez & Paul Tran. You witnessed these poems as they began.

And to my dear friend & collaborator, Joël Díaz for your warmth & support, and for your late-night FaceTime calls & lipsynchs. You've taught me so much through your softness and spirit.

From the get-go, Ariel Goldberg, Paolo Javier, and Lara Mimosa Montes, y'all have believed in my words & images. I'm grateful for the kindness & camaraderie you've shown me.

And to my pamilya, dito at sa Pilipinas. Mama, Papa, Ate Amy, Ate Analyn, Kuya Archie, Aileen at mga bulilit mo. To RJ & Rachelle. SALAMAT. SALAMAT.

Aldrin Valdez is a Pinoy writer and visual artist. They grew up in Manila and Long Island and currently live in Brooklyn. Aldrin has been awarded fellowships from Queer/Art/Mentorship and Poets House. Their poetry & visual art appear in *The Felt, Femmescapes, Nat Brut, Poor Claudia,* and *The Recluse.* Aldrin has also presented work at Dixon Place, The Metropolitan Museum of Art, and The Poetry Project. Collaborating with writer & organizer Ted Kerr, Aldrin co-curated Foundational Sharing, a salon series of readings, performances, & visual art. Most recently, they've co-curated two seasons of the Segue Reading Series with fellow poet Joël Díaz.

Nightboat Books

Nightboat Books, a nonprofit organization, seeks to develop audiences for writers whose work resists convention and transcends boundaries. We publish books rich with poignancy, intelligence, and risk. Please visit our website, www.nightboat.org, to learn about our titles and how you can support our future publications.

The following individuals have supported the publication of this book. We thank them for their generosity and commitment to the mission of Nightboat Books:

Kazim Ali
Anonymous
Photios Giovanis
Elenor & Thomas Kovachevich
Elizabeth Motika
Leslie Scalapino — O Books Fund
Benjamin Taylor
Jerrie Whitfield & Richard Motika

In addition, this book has been made possible, in part, by grants from the National Endowment for the Arts and the New York State Council on the Arts Literature Program.